Citizenship

Being a Leader

Cassie Mayer

Heinemann Library
Chicago, Illinois

© 2008 Heinemann Library
an imprint of Capstone Global Library, LLC
Chicago, Illinois

Customer Service 888-454-2279
Visit our website at www.heinemannraintree.com

Designed by Joanna Hinton-Malivoire
Illustrated by Mark Beech
Printed and bound in China by Leo Paper Group.

11
10 9 8 7 6 5 4

The Library of Congress has cataloged the first edition of this book as follows:
Mayer, Cassie.
  Being a leader / Cassie Mayer.
      p. cm. -- (Citizenship)
  Includes bibliographical references and index.
  ISBN 978-1-4034-9486-3 (hc) -- ISBN 978-1-4034-9494-8 (pbk.) 1. Leadership--Juvenile literature. I. Title.
  BF637.L4M393 2007
  158'.4--dc22
                                    2006039387

Contents

Being a leader means taking charge.

Being a leader means setting
a good example.

When you help someone …

you are being a good leader.

When you take charge ...

you are being a good leader.

When you invite others to
join in ...

you are being a good leader.

When you help others with
a problem …

you are being a good leader.

When you praise others ...

you are being a good leader.

When you keep trying …

you are being a good leader.

When you give others a turn
to lead …

you are being a good leader.

It is important to be a good leader.

How can you be a good leader?

Activity

How is this child being a good leader?

Picture Glossary

 **leader** someone who takes charge

 **praise** to tell someone you think they did a good job

Index

Note to Parents and Teachers
Each book in this series shows examples of behavior that demonstrate good citizenship. Take time to discuss each illustration and ask children to identify the leadership skills shown. Use the question on page 21 to ask students how they can be good leaders.

The text has been chosen with the advice of a literacy expert to enable beginning readers success while reading independently or with moderate support. You can support children's nonfiction literacy skills by helping them use the table of contents, picture glossary, and index.